enjoy

Strict Forms

by the Barking Foxes

 New Generation Publishing

This book has been produced with assistance from
The London Borough of Barking and Dagenham Library Service
Pen to Print Creative Writing Project 2017/8
with funding from
The Arts Council, England Grants for the Arts.

Over the course of two years, the Barking Foxes Poetry Stanza has studied a different form of poetry every month.

Whilst grappling with the usual creative process, it has been challenging and exciting to see the fruits of such an academic pursuit.

Some of the chapters have several entries and some have fewer. It is actually quite difficult to just sit down and decide to write a sestina. As anyone who writes will attest, it is quite difficult to sit down and write anything some days.

This anthology has been written by members of the Barking Foxes Poetry Stanza, we hope you enjoy this selection.

Contents

Chapter 1 - Haiku

A traditional Japanese haiku is a three-line poem with seventeen syllables, written in a 5/7/5 syllable count. Often focusing on images from nature, haiku emphasizes simplicity, intensity, and directness of expression.

Haiku began in thirteenth-century Japan as the opening phrase of renga, an oral poem, generally 100 stanzas long. The much shorter haiku broke away from renga in the sixteenth-century, and was mastered a century later by Matsuo Basho, who wrote haiku sometimes using 3/4/5 syllables.

Haiku is traditionally written in the present tense and focused on associations between images.

Don't worry if when someone says "Haiku! and you get the urge to respond with "Bless You?"

Warning, Haiku writing can become addictive!

Anyone with a yellow coat

Hearing of a friend's sudden death

Will knit a black shawl

by Jenny Grant

*

Forgotten willow

bending gracefully its neck.

Time to sleep.

by Agnieszka Dryjas-Makhloufi

*

The tranquil morning

holds joy in the light bringing

Each morn, hope renewed

by Mary L Walsh

*

Cunning Odysseus, wooden horse

Siege of many years

Walls breached, fair Helen captured

by Jenny Grant

*

I hang out odd socks
Wonder where their partners go
Lost in the ether?

by Mary L Walsh

*

Sweet cherry orchard
dancing wildly in the rain.
The moon peeps through twigs

By Agnieszka Dryjas-Makhloufi

*

He wondered if he
bought her a rose of blood red
would she be willing?

by Mary L Walsh

*

Bleak white sky, no birds, silence
Cold house, pen scratches
Who'd believe magic lingers

by Jenny Grant

*

Sunlight glitters during rain

Dark clouds part sharply

Birds sing as we leave

by Jenny Grant

*

Sinking in the pond

a beautifully decorated boat

sings its last song.

By Agnieszka Dryjas-Makhloufi

*

Long black tail feather on path

Trees part let us pass

Grey sky, low clouds, damp afternoon

by Jenny Grant

*

Texting not talking

without talking or walking

just a bum with thumbs

By Mary L. Walsh

*

Chapter 2 - Villanelle

If you love a highly structured form of poetry with a rigid rhyme scheme, then the Villanelle may be for you.

It is made up of 19 lines, two repeating lines and two refrains. The first and third lines of the opening tercet are repeated alternately in the succeeding stanzas.

This poetry form originated during the Renaissance in Italian and Spanish dance songs on a pastoral theme. An excellent example of this is Dylan Thomas "Do Not Go Gentle Into That Good Night."

Bomber

by Jenny Grant

I lied and said I didn't know you
To the FBI agents at my door
It was such a shock when I heard about the bomb

I figured I had two days before they came back
Heard about it on the news the day before
So, I lied and said I didn't know you

I sat down to write about the time we'd spent together
I'd have loved to see you once more
It was a shock to hear about the bomb

About Maria, and the fall from the fire escape
I had time to think how you broke the law
I just lied and said I didn't know you

The books you'd written would never be finished
You fought the establishment tooth and claw
It was a shock to hear about the bomb

I put it all down, everything I knew about you
Terrorism filled your every pore
Yet I lied and said I didn't know you
It was a shock to hear about the bomb

A Song from Scottish Mountains

By Agnieszka Dryjas-Makhloufi

In the heart of an old oak beneath the bark
a song about olden days slowly flows.
Plish plop plish plop coming out of the dark.

On slender oak branches a lonely lark
listens curiously as the east wind blows
in the heart of an old oak beneath the bark.

Shepherds whistle at their lost sheep. Hark! Hark!
Through the wet bushes hungry wolf 's eye glows.
Plish plop plish plop coming out of the dark.

A song about a she-wolf and young lad
can be heard along with the mountain woes
in the heart of an old oak beneath the bark.

A young lad's heart is sinking in his wark.
After losing his lover, his tear rolls.
Plish plop plish plop coming out of the dark.

The night unbuttons her brocaded sark,
murmurs softly kissing the drowsy rose.
In the heart of an old oak beneath the bark.
Plish plop plish plop coming out of the dark.

Market Villanelle

by Mary L Walsh

The market stalls in colours bright and bold
Offer goods and chattels of the age
Display their beauteous wonders to behold

Here in brightly coloured folds
"Two for a pound!" the trader on his stage
The market stalls in colours bright and bold

Customers come to pick and choose and hold
Their bargain prizes won to don the age
Display the beauteous wonders to behold

In domestic settings to behold
To ape celebrity on "Hello's" page
At market stalls in colours bright and bold

Then dressed in such array bright and bold
They don their make up as if upon the stage
To display the beauteous wonder to behold

They visit once again to fit the mould
Of Essex girl or boy upon the street
The market stalls in colours bright and bold
Display their beauteous wonders to behold

Chapter 3 - Cento

This form of poetry can be highly rewarding and produce some surprising results. Its name means "Patchwork" and it is exactly that, a poem made up from lines of another poet's work.

Pick lines and then manipulate them into telling a new story. It is customary to acknowledge the poets work you have used.

Famous examples of this: "The Dong with the Luminous Nose" by John Ashbury or Peter Gizzi's "Ode Salute to the New York School.

Ten Thousand Miles of Farewell - from poems by Li Po

by Jenny Grant

Ten thousand miles of farewell on this boat
and no-one knows where you've gone; still
I sit silent. All bottomless clarity.
Here, the world's dust rinsed from my face
I set my hair loose among pine winds

But we're not made with such ancestral chi
so how long can we wander with it here?
I sit, heart stricken, at the bloom of youth
in my old face. Return to clear water
and a blossoming moon bares our delusions

A restless woman cries out in half-sleep
A lit path of white stretches between us
Ocean clouds leave the eyes farewell
Western light follows water away. Once gone,
gone without a trace.

Those who could hear a song this deeply
Vanished long ago.

The Fate of Erin

by Mary L Walsh

Wretched Erin with what grief I see
The fatal changes time has made in thee
the excuse, what blindness caused it?
That bias in your indirections?
Is courage in a maiden's breast
Less pleasing than in a man?
An evil world is now at hand
In which men shall be in bondage and women free.
I could scale the blue air
I could plough the high hills
Or plant a wreath from the banks of that river
The heart, the harp that are sleeping forever

All verses taken from the "Penguin Book of Irish Poetry" edited by Patrick Crotty

1   Verses occasioned by the sudden drying up of St Patrick's Well, Trinity college, Dublin Jonathan Swift (30 November 1667 – 19 October 1745)

2   The Curse. Robin Flower 1881-1946 ; b. 16 Oct.,;

3   Amazonian Gift – Dorothea Dubois

4   World Gone Wrong   Standish Hayes O'Grady 19/05/1832 – 16/10/1915

5   Dark Rosaleen – JC Mangan   James Clarence Mangan (Irish: Séamus Ó Mangáin; 1 May 1803, Dublin – 20 June 1849),

6   Goujane Barra-Jeremiah Joseph Callanan 1795-1829

Fears

By Agnieszka Dryjas-Makhloufi – with lines from an anthology of
poetry

I dream of someday touching the sky.
My eyes glisten with tears.
The coldness reaches my heart.
I am afraid, oh I am so afraid!
All my dreams may not come true.

I spent my time hiding out from the world.
But the time has now come to conquer my fears.
So I chase away thoughts – stinging wasps
and come into the presence of still water.

Chapter 4 - Split Poem

A split poem is a novel way of creating a poem utilising some existing text, which you deconstruct and reimagine using your own words.

Apparently split poems began to appear during the height of the artistic movement in the early part of the 20th Century known as Surrealism. Surrealist poets liked to write in a challenging way, and enjoyed being deliberately shocking and absurd.

Split poems afford a technique whereby you can juxtapose contrasting images and words to great effect, and you can amp up or tone down the dissonance you are provoking from your readers.

To create a split poem, take a piece of writing from any source, it can be as diverse as a science textbook, a magazine article about a politician, or a page from a favourite novel; then you write some of the words in groups down one side of a sheet of paper. Then, using your own words, you start or finish the lines freely incorporating you have appropriated, and like alchemy, you then end up with a piece of writing which is entirely your own.

Using this technique, you will find the end results surprising, and it's quite a satisfying way to write a poem.

The Last Ties

by Jenny Grant

Here at the age of forty-nine I began to be old. My last love had died.
I waited at the foot of the metal bridge for you; the three of us who
  loved you.
I knew it all, the whole drab compass of marital disillusionment.
Seeing the coldness between you, the continual disappointment.

Nothing remained to you except the chill bonds of law and duty.
You belong elsewhere, away from me, I've had enough of you, she
  said.
A mood of aloofness and cold criticism broke the last ties,
Things you took from me, the money you wasted, the absences.

The hard set at the corners of her mouth told you nothing
You never saw me as I was, she said. I showed you all my colours.
The nervous trick with the fingers when you were lying.
I only wanted you to see me as I really am, she said; you couldn't
  even do that.

Reflecting the Clouds

by Jenny Grant

At the age when my eyes were dry to all
save poetry, I wept often
but never for you. I repented
my folly, you broke me.
It was your chief sport.
You denied me any comfort.
Tell someone else you said.

You slept soundly while I lay
awake, fretting. You were the kind
of man I could not trust with the simplest duty
If I got on the wrong side of you
you'd take it out of me in other ways.
I was only thirteen when you pushed me down a hill.
I still see the scar.

You made it awkward for me
with my mother. She feasted on mouldy cake
next to a broken vase and padlocked door.
There were rotten eggs in the kitchen
bin bags piled along the hall
Your house was left in a disgraceful condition.
I cried for you.

Mother worried
about the leaves on the lawn.
She asked me to take down the branches that overhang.
If I could do something with a purpose
I would get more cheerful, she said.
All I wanted was to reflect the clouds
and the mighty beech trees.

Days to Come

by Jenny Grant

Days to come
I'll look back over these times
Think on how you rode hard
through my pain and suffering.
You were a mountain
turned your back against me
like a barren wind gap, closed to the sky.

I sat the horses among the rocks,
they dwelt in silence.
And I looked out over the country
to the south, towards the other place,
I was so far from my home.
The last shadows of my heart
were running over the land.

Before the wind set to work
on my shame and my disappointments
my face turned red and I cried
at the memory. But the sun
to the west spoke of home and of joy.
I ran among the shelving cloud
high up on the mesa.

The distant cordilleras speak
to me of my family, of those I love now.
I can't help but be overcome with gladness
to have found such a place,
ranged down from the terminals of the sky.
To fade from pale, to pale of blue
and then to nothing at all.

The Assassin

by Jenny Grant

In the darkest part of the night
in the comfort and the closeness
the assassin came over the wall into the garden.
Can I show you my secrets?

He ran noiselessly for the front
of the stone fortress of the universe inside
and stopped short of the soaring walls.
My soul, you play with me

Leaving me broken and happy and dazed
deftly he threw a cloth covered hook
into the shining gladness
with a thin silk rope attached to my love.

Dare I give my heart to you?
You, in your close fitting black clothes
you're perfectly in tune with me
the drama and the passion.

The hook caught the stone ledge
of the embrasure.
Was I dreaming as I fell?
Your innermost workings, we're music

He shinned up the rope, oh the smiles we shared
The splendour of you, silent.
He squeezed through the slit
and disappeared inside.

Chapter 5 - Sonnet

Shakespeare liked the poetry form so much he wrote 154! One of the most famous sonnets is Sonnet 18 "Shall I compare thee to a summer's day"

A sonnet, in English poetry, is a poem of fourteen lines, usually in iambic pentameter, a line of verse with five metrical feet, each consisting of one short (or unstressed) syllable followed by one long (or stressed) syllable, for example Two households, both alike in dignity.- although there are a couple of exceptions, and years of experimentation that have loosened this definition.

How to write a Sonnet

1. Use the Shakespearean rhyme scheme. ...

2. Write your lines in iambic pentameter. ...

3. Vary your meter from time to time. ...

4. Follow the Shakespearean sonnet's stanzaic structure. ...

5. Develop your stanzas thoughtfully. ...

6. Choose your subject matter carefully. ...

7. Write your Shakespearean sonnet.

Sonnet of Old Age - (Shakespearian style)

by Elizabeth Freeman

The glittering days of childhood fade and wane
The memory clouds, deceives, and goes away
Then, like a miracle, returns again.
Though some harp back towards a happier day.
So, what of age?   What can we say of this?
The culmination of an active life?
Some look on age as endless days of bliss,
With rest and peace, inactive, free from strife.
O hear my words, spoken with aging voice
Silent so long, now speaking from the heart.
Age creeps along, and grasps us, without choice,
Giving us time to gaze, as recompense.
O learn to live with joy and endless love
To those around, and most, - to God above.

Roses are...

By Eithne Cullen

Roses I'm told are red and violets blue
but red is for danger, we know it's so,
for blood and birth and battle's gory hue;
it's for anger and passion's fiery glow.
Red is in cherries, apples: harvest stores.
Red is in glowing firelight, sunset skies.
We dream of blue skies, calm and restful shores:
indigo innocence in babies' eyes.
Blue is a mood, a calm and restful shade.
When you are down, they say you've got the blues:
twelve bar rhythms hauntingly being played;
Sinatra's eyes and Elvis Presley's shoes.
There are so many shades of red and blue
The shades of meaning - what they'd mean to you.

Sonnet

by Lucy Kaufman

Love, if one thing is removed, is not Love
If one thing is added, cannot be Love.
As true as math's, Love is a pure spring,
Distilled to its very essence, a Nobel Prize
winner could pin it like a butterfly
to the periodic table, where we would worship
its atomic beauty aspire to its unique ideals.
If replicated, there would be no need for vows.
In truth, the years turn the spring into a muddy brook,
Iced over in Winter, parched in the Summer months.
What was once thirst-quenching takes on the taste
of all that water under the bridge, seasoned
by rusty pram spokes, dumped tyres, canvas and pains,
A contraption that serves as an umbrella, of sorts, when it rains.

Spring Sonnet

by Mary L Walsh

Now the garden comes to life in bloom
Sprouting, burgeoning life springs green and new
With promises of colours seen from room
Filling up the senses as it grew

These tender plants are nurtured from the gloom
Of winters darkness into spring anew
And summer pushes in through the rain and looms
Above our heads, the sun dispels the dew

Clouds run from its beams, earth dons costume
Of vivid greens, pale yellow, reds and blues
From earth springs life like babies from the womb
Beds golden, red and filled with violets blue

Stretch before the eye to meet sky blue
Completing the picture, earth renewed.

Farm Cat

By Eithne Cullen

The farm cat, linen white with ginger patches,
pauses on the grassy bank and watches.
Stares into the tangles, as the grass twitches;
still as a stone, his keen eye fixes.

Becomes a thing of feline sound and vision,
homing in with surgical precision.
The careless mouse, darting, unaware.
Spotted by the hunter, its end is near.

Now, realising its fate: heart thumping,
no time to hide, the cat already jumping,
plucking him from any chance of retreat,
this is not sport, this one is to eat.

Victorious, the long-tailed victim in his jaws.
An ordered farm yard ruled by jungle laws.

Sonnet about Love

by Agnieszka Dryjas-Makhloufi

Oh, lovely lady, oh lovely lady!
I am waiting for thee, I am not a liar.
Calling thy name, I smell of a daisy
I watch thee dress by the ball of fire.

Thou make me gasp for breath, in despair
drink from the deep fountain of thy goodness.
I kiss thy branches like my lover's hair
Thou art mine shelter in my poorness.

Oh dear! I shall come to thee every night
to say my prayers and at the dawn
kiss my wonderful princess like a knight.
My feelings to thee will never be gone.

Oh, thou art raindrops, thou art gold! I claim:
Nature! Nature! Nature! That's thy name!

Man Talk

by H.B. O'Neill

Alright?

Yeah.

How's yer mum?

Ugh. Chemo.

Oh.

Yeah.

Tough.

Yeah.

Sorry.

Yeah. Not your fault.

Ha. No.

Thanks though.

Yeah.

See ya.

Sonnet to a Spotted Cat

by Jenny Grant

Little cat, you with the quizzical brow
How your long legs whiz down the garden path
Bring me a dying starling and miaow
Chase it round as I watch you from the bath

Your fur is white, and once it was quite clean
But you like rolling in a patch of dirt
Your paws are pink and black, your eyes are green
Leave grey footprints on my clean white shirt

You have stolen my heart you little beast
I can't sleep unless you are by my feet
I long for your love but you love me least
You have conquered me, I admit defeat

Dear Spottie, independent, wild and free
If I keep feeding you, will you love me?

Sonnet for a Lovely Man

By Mary L Walsh

I saw you in the Barge Aground just drinking ale
Tall, standing by the bar and laughing free
I watched your face as you retold a tale
And saw your mates smiling there with glee

Noisy drinking broke in with the sound
of clinking glasses, filled then swiftly cleared
The question asked with cheer "Another round? "
Was greeted with applause and swiftly downed

Ben Sherman shirt and denim stay- pressed jeans
Confident in manner and in poise
I loved you then, young, strong, handsome and lean
You've proved that love can conquer all the noise

For forty years and more time gave us joy and tears
My lovely man, I've loved you through the years.

Chapter 6 - Ekphrastic Poetry

If picture paints a thousand words, then the Ekphrastic form may be for you.

It is simply poetry inspired by art.

Becoming Rothko

by Jenny Grant

I am quite at peace
Gentle light scatters the gloom from my heart
Around me, I can sense strangers moving in circles.

Unable to harness the stillness
They're rushing past the glorious colours
Eyes open, but not seeing.

My soul is open so wide in front of you
We speak in paint marks, canvas, heartbreak
I am in the center of the universe, becoming something else.

"The Windmills at Vaan Daam" by Claude Monet

By Mary L Walsh

Sails that turn for static purpose creak
Through the yellowing dawn as waters lap
Upon the grassy bank reeds anchor, deep
Into the muddy silt which sucks and saps
While boatmen wait for sun to crack and creak
Across the brightening sky's dappled wispy clouds
Emboldens birds to take to yellowed air
Their cries emit a keening, haunting sound
As oars splash into waters fair
Breaking the reflections held there
The windmill sails the turn to grind and mill
The sails upon the boats are hauled aloft
The day begins its toil, a grinding thrill
Of promised riches earned and fortunes lost.

Tell Not Show

by H.B. O'Neill Inspired by Reubens Rainbow Landscape

"Rainbow."
"No."
"No?"
"No."
"No?"
"No. Never say rainbow in a poem. It's a no no."
"Oh."

Father and Son

by Agnieszka Dryjas-Makhloufi
Inspired by "The Hay Wain" by J. Constable

The trees sway in the air
drinking in the serenity.
Twigs caress the house roof
and then sink in the sunrays.
Dogs' barking breaks the silence
and cuts the sky into two.
Horses with heavy hooves
drag the carriage.
A long way behind them.
Still a long way ahead of them.
Father and son in anticipation of
mouthful of supper.
Their minds swirl
like their carriage wheels.
Sinister clouds gather above them.
The wind howls into their ears
like a lone wolf.

Pictures that's Laura's

by Robert Drury inspired by the paintings of Laura I

1. Modern contemporary art fires on all fours,
    In the dark matter world where Indigo's drawn.
    From the depths of Death's dank old dreams,
    there springs forth brand new Life, and so it seems.

2. Some people in business are known to be so glum.
    Conservative strictures bang the same old beat drum.
    Those who want to keep life's pride right in, at least
    may now face a new artistic challenging masterpiece.

3. Must all the world be at war with us all?
    Can we not see the beauty, that can walk so tall?
    In life there is strife, to create an honoured life.
    Making nice we like, but do we need that strife?

4. The desire to create above the current moral slaughter
    demands from the artist, spiritual growth to really water.
    Breaking out of our mental comfort zone lines,
    This new life pours forth where Laura so shines

5. Creation in heart and mind finds ways to brighten our living,
    with paintings to support our challenging metaphysical reasoning.
    We start with art that has a free life that we can think on.
    So, get with the collection, who brings it this season.

6. The world does not know it just as yet, of course.
   But come the day, it will come to know, this fine cause.
   Out of the world painted in dark indigo restraint
   blooms the wild Garden of Eden in vivid paint.

7. Drawing in from mystic regions, the spirit of mankind
   connects to the unknown and then be shown what to find.
   Living artist meets metamorphic minds to bring us that find
   who then makes it up in the way for us to follow that fine line.

8. The universal living world of natural beauty really exists
   In the Spiritual World where God keeps it to persist.
   The Garden of Eden is seen, these truly mystical righteous lands,
   waiting for us to walk in its ways, tended by His bold hands.

9. Again and again, Laura retraces her mighty steps.
   Again and again, the Garden of Eden flowers best
   when shaped and painted with Laura's skillful finger,
   then viewed and mused, let us appreciate, as we linger.

10. Daisy chaining flower power dancing in great light,
    Spin the wheel of love to light the heart to be so bright.
    Growth in thick paint develops growth in great hope.
    Let it grow, let it flow my friends, let us see the show.

11. Pushing up boundaries within our dear thin souls,
    Searching up and down in the creative mould.
    From deep in the wonderful world that is to unfurl
    A flowering of painted nature, that is been shown.

12. There is something new for everyone out there to see,
    Laura even paints a new dress in solid paint, for us to be free.
    The extraordinary, the implausible, becomes quite plausible,
    the heart at the centre of life's beat to give it causality.

13. While Eve was God's crowning glory to behold with beauty,
    Why rip a good thing down, when there is love is in it, truly.
    Laura portrays, The Eve waring that Love in the Garden
    Be we Adam? Can we step to the art to be a soul master?

14. The inventive expressionism, the thoughts passed across.
    Fashioning that expression, waring this art form, of course,
    is a walk in the blooming good garden of flowers with Eve.
    So, enjoy this expression from where you are, if so you believe.

15. The passion to organise an exploration to Impossible inventiveness
    requires technical innovation and extravagant courageousness.
    To meditate while connected to the living discovering truth,
    Let us celebrate an overwhelming ecstatic breakthrough, if true.

16. Thinking outside the box gets you joining right in the box
    of fashionable out of the ordinary thoughts stuck in your box.
    There, happily developing assuredly, pictorial ways, mentally
    fought.
    A smearing here, a scraping there, digesting an ageing idea, so
    caught.

17. From all the work put in by Laura, art has a master of paint a shape,
    A free expressional world of vivid multi-coloured canvas assurance.
    A radical collective in three dimensional tactile paint.
    Free thought together, we ride our dream without restraint.

18. Drawing power from within the emotive focus,
    enigmatically feeding on the emotive lotus.
    Let's go reaching for dimensions without numbers.
    discovering dimensions without number.

That's the pictures that's Laura's.

Chapter 7 - How-to Poems

Some poems explain a procedure, or how to do something.

It might be directions on how to play a game or make a craft or even do something silly like making an ENORMOUS snowman.

Line-by-line, such poems walk readers through a process and teach them to do something new.

How to Tickle a Trout

by H.B. O'Neill

Approach with appropriate apprehension
Fixate with fiery focus
Stretch with stealthy sinew
Reach with reactionary relish

(If you must)

Ha!
Topple like a tiresome toddler
Splash like spurned sputum
Flounder flummoxed filcher

Hey, Poacher! leave them fish alone!

How to Hunt the Shellakybookie

by Mary L Walsh

Go into the garden just as twilight breaks
Do not be afraid
Of crocodiles and snakes
The beast you hunt is cunning
But not a carnivore
There's no fear of being eaten
As you scan the garden floor.
Look first for a silver trail
For foliage chewed and broken
Search with a torch behind the pots
'Tis there you'll find lots and lots.
When you have found your quarry
Spiral shelled with perfect coil
Clustered with companions
Above the dank dark soil
Approach stealthily and grasp with fingers
the Shellakybookie house
Or please use tweezers
If you are timid as a mouse.
Then once firm grip is taken
its suction hold is broken
Launch him up and over
Into next doors garden
Repeat this process time and again
'til in your neighbour's field they are creeping
If spotted have an alibi
Just tell them you were sleeping!

How to be Happy

by Agnieszka Dryjas- Makhloufi

Take a dose of sunlight.
Kiss rose petals
on your way home.
Sink in the sunset
and dance in the pond.

Have a walk in a forest,
listen to its breath.
Talk to your beloved ones.
Wear your smile
even if it's the only
thing you have.

When a bunch of problems arrive
sit and listen to your heart.
In despair and anger
see a beautiful way out.
Just embrace the whole experience.
There will be more good to come.

Sultana Loaf Heaven

By Jenny Grant

Go into the kitchen and pick out your favourite mug.
One you drink out of each day, you like the feel of. Fill your
mug with sultanas and tip into a sizeable pan, not a soup
pan but a solid and sturdy pan you might cook potatoes in.

Add half a mug of sugar and a full mug of milk, sprinkle in
some nutmeg or cinnamon, it will perfume your house.
Cut off a big chunk of butter and add that in, give it a proper stir.
My Nanny used to put in a tiny knob of butter, her cake was dry.

We're not on diets and it's a cake recipe for God's sake.

Make sure all your ingredients are stirred and set it to boil
This cake needs a proper scalding, it's a boiled cake
My Great Grandmother used to make this cake for her family.
My Grandad loved it; I make this always for the love of him.

Once it's boiling loudly, look at the clock and let it seethe
for four minutes. Don't worry if it burns a bit, it turns into
caramel and tastes great. Grandad always liked these
ones best, the ones I thought I'd ruined by not watching.

Turn it off and let it cool. Do not eat the hot mixture,
your mouth will catch fire, and you will curse me.
Warn errant family members to steer clear also
with their naughty probing fingers and spoons.

They might not listen. You might need to guard the mixture.

When you get up to turn the cake mixture off, the house will smell
of vanilla and spices. Milky steam might cloud up your windows,
and when stirring the pan, you'll see the sultanas have been transmuted
into fat golden cabochons, set in an opalescent custard sauce.

After an hour or so, the mixture will have cooled. You will then be safe
to add a couple of eggs and a mug of flour. If you really love someone,
break a big bar of dairy milk into the mixture. The squat gobbins of
  chocolate
melt slightly during cooking but they never solidify entirely again.

You won't regret the chocolate. Glace cherries are also a wise choice.

Stir it all about. Bake in a loaf tin at Gas Mark 3 for an hour. Oh the
fragrance in my hair and on my skin. This cake can be utterly
  breathtaking.
Be careful who you give it to; you might create slaves with this.
Choose wisely. Those who eat it should be deserving of its sticky
  perfection.

It's quite a sexy cake really, one for lovers, and honey trappers.

How to Garden on a Sunny Day

By Mary L Walsh

First the essentials
Get out of bed
Before 8 a.m. the experts have said
Then get dressed in old clothes
and tatty old shoes, just fit for gardening
and for no other use.

Now go through your house
Or your flat or your barn
Pause only to put on the kettle
Then sit in your garden, coffee in hand
to plan on which part you will settle.

Once half an hour or so has passed
Get the tools from the shed you may need for your task
A spade and a fork, a hoe and a rake,
a trowel and a dibber, holes for to make
a bucket or pail for composting sake.

Approach now the bed that is all growing wild
The weeds are resisting, like a petulant child
They must be pulled up but you need to decide,
which are weeds and which are flowers
Even to Google this may really take
Hours and hours and hours.

At about 10.30 you may need a break
And the coffee pot calls long and low
Find and arbour or a sunny nook
Where you can sip coffee and eat toast,
While simultaneously reading a book

You may find now
That time has flown
And lunch time is calling your name
By 1pm it is getting too warm
to continue this gardening game
you may sit with a salad or compose a ballad
Until the heat wanes again.

You cannot take the risk
When the weather's like this
Of sunstroke or sunburn or worse
Retreat to the shade in the heat of the day
Mad dogs will ignore this.

By 4 in the noon you can resume
planting marigolds, geraniums and pansies
make a hole in the earth
to fit the plants girth
to spread colour along with the daisies

Water them well
'Til the ground does swell and
is rich with dampness and lime
At the end of the day put all tools away

Wait now for the passage of time
Light citronella candles immediately
to stop the bugs from biting
survey your hard work in the flickering lighting
Now open the wine
Sit, sip, and dine
Tomorrow continue the fighting!

How to Mend Your Broken Heart

By Jenny Grant

Take a deep breath and dab your eyes with a tissue.
Try to stop sobbing; your chest is probably hurting.
Put both hands to your ribcage and feel your heart beating
in your chest. Listen to its rhythm under your fingers.

Speak these words gently to your poor broken heart: "Dear
heart of mine, I know you've been broken into a hundred pieces.
I'm here with you and I'll look after you. I'll wait with you
until the feelings of panic and disappointment subside a bit."

Breathe some more. Think brave thoughts.
If you've been crying a lot, go and get a cup of tea
or a nice glass of water. Try to sit still and focus
on taking gentle sips and try to enjoy the silence in the room.

Go and wash your face. You're not the first person
to be let down. Breathe. Smile at your reflection
in the bathroom mirror. If your face is red
and puffy you might even make yourself chuckle.

Think of something nice to do, something you can do
for yourself to make you feel better. Once I cried throughout
a whole head of highlights and a cut and blow dry.
I gave the hairdresser a big tip. She didn't mind.

Chapter 8 - Ballad

Ballads have a long history and are found in many cultures. The ballad actually began as a folk song and continues today in popular music. Many love songs today can be considered ballads.

A typical ballad consists of stanzas that contain a quatrain, or four poetic lines. The meter or rhythm of each line is usually iambic, which means it has one unstressed syllable followed by a stressed syllable. In ballads, there are usually eight or six syllables in a line.

Like any poem, some ballads follow this form and some don't, but almost all ballads are narrative, which means they tell a story.

Because the ballad was originally set to music, some ballads have a refrain, or a repeated chorus, just like a song does. Similarly, the rhyme scheme is often ABAB because of the musical quality of this rhyme pattern.

While ballads have always been popular, it was during the Romantic movement of poetry in the late 18th century that the ballad had resurgence and became a popular form. Many famous romantic poets, like William Wordsworth, wrote in the ballad form.

The Traveler's Ballad

By Mary L Walsh

The Traveler searched for better life
Across the sea with rolling waves
He found the city life so strange
Missed his mother's loving ways

The Traveler searched for any work
in this unfriendly land
"No Irish need apply" they said
When he asked for work at hand

The Traveler worked on tarmacked roads
To earn his crust of bread
The sights and songs of Ireland
circled gently in his head

No more a stranger in this land
His family followed on
As years rolled by, he settled in
The emptiness long gone

Returning to his native land
When age had taken hold
The traveler saw in black and white
Memories he'd gilded gold.

Ballad of S.S. Roumania

by Elizabeth Freeman

The ship sailed off from Liverpool
In 1892.
A mother waved, and watched her son
Until he went from view.

She'd come back home from India,
For she had been so ill.
In fact her husband wrote and said,
"You should wait longer still."

"I'm coming home to fetch you soon,
And I will take you back.
So stay there with the children now,
And maybe start to pack."

She did not heed his good advice,
Her health was now OK.
Her duty was to be with him.
So she was on her way.

She told her children of her plan,
Their little faces fell.
So sorry to be losing her,
But glad that she was well.

The children begged and pleaded,
"Whatever will we do?
How will we manage here alone?
We really do need you."

"My children, you will have to learn
To manage without me.
I'm returning to your father
Across the bright blue sea."

When her son got home to Ireland
He gave the children sweets
That were given by their mother
As a parting little treat.

A few days later, at breakfast,
Whilst pouring out the tea.
One read the news headlines –
"AN APPALLING CATASTROPHE".

"ROUMANIA" wrecked off Portugal.
"That's Mother's ship", they cried.
Their faces paled, and each one thought,
Had their poor mother died?

In stony silence they all sat
Staring at each other,
Just stunned, and silenced by the thought,
That they had lost their mother.

Unsay those words, turn back the clock,
It surely cannot be,
That steamship Roumania
Had been wrecked by the sea.

Two days after leaving England
There was a most ferocious gale.
No one on board knew where they were,
Or which way they should sail.

Their bearings they completely lost,
And did not cast their lead.[led]
They sailed due South, instead of East,
Nor saw the land ahead.

Meanwhile the passengers aboard,
Were struggling for their lives,
Drowning like rats in a dark hole,
Families, husbands, wives.

Their mother's cabin was on deck,
Four ladies shared the room.
They ran outside when the ship struck,
And into the saloon.

An Army captain was in there,
He lived to tell the tale.
A huge wave smashed the saloon down,
Such was the violent gale.

Its back-wash dragged the ladies out
Into the treacherous ocean.
The next wave tossed them on the ship,
Which stunned them with this motion.

The man got wedged in the saloon,
Then flung out on a wave.
And landing on the sand nearby
Escaped the watery grave.

The children's mother was washed up
On Foz, a sandy beach.,
And buried in a church yard near,
That's within easy reach.

"My children, you will have to learn
To manage without me."
They hear their mother's words again
From deep beneath the sea.

Over the Rivers, over the Hills

by Agnieszka Dryjas- Makhloufi

Over the rivers, over the hills
a beautiful girl lives.
The wind echoes the girl's song.

In the evening wolves' enchanted hearts beat.
Watching the moonlight, they put cubs to sleep.
The wind echoes the girl's song.

A tired shepherd seeking the shelter
halts fascinated by the voice of the belter.
The wind echoes the girl's song.

'Where is the voice coming from?' – I wonder.
The trees sway a few miles yonder.
The wind echoes the girl 's song.

Ballad Of The Sea Woman

by Elizabeth Freeman

A cottage roofed with ageing thatch
clung to the rocky shore,
Sea pinks, in numerous bunches, grew
in clusters round the door.

Each year more strands of thatch blew off,
though anchored down by stones,
yet still the leaking roof defied
the strong winds howling moans.

Old Dilly lived where she was born.
Sea music in her ears.
Sea women sang, and waved to her,
companions many years.

She'd sit there on her favourite rock,
long arms waved from the foam.
She saw their faces, heard them laugh,
and heard their gentle moan.

Child folk who danced upon the sand,
sang softly in the spray.
Sea mist, sea breath, enveloped them,
and carried them away.

At night she heard them crooning.
The shining stars above.
Sea women's children calling me,
my children, who I love.

She would gather moss and seaweed,
lay them out on rocks to dry,
then tie them up in bunches
to sell to passers-by.

She watched the cormorant spread its wings,
and heard the curlew's cry.
Seagulls calling, swooping, diving,
flocks of birds flew by.

Driftwood and gorse to light her fire.
Fresh fish to eat each day.
Leaks and draughts never bothered her.
Her heart was in the bay.

Now, Mrs Gregg was most concerned.
"Her house is falling down,
Old Dilly should be moved out fast
and go to live in town."

This lady had brought change before,
to families, young and old,
and even pigs been moved from homes
to sties out in the cold.

"You know I never interfere,
but leave this up to me,
if someone doesn't help her soon,
she'll just float out to sea."

A sanitary inspector came.
His verdict – "House condemned.
The workhouse, or a village home,
is what we recommend."

Trembling, she drew her shawl around.
He saw her haunting eyes.
Something about her touched his heart.
"Let's gently break her ties."

"When your men strip the thatch, she'll leave,
I see no other way,"
"We can't do that.   Speak to the priest,
And see what he can say."

Afraid and threatened, Dilly shook,
and trembled violently.
The priest was troubled at her plight,
"Come Dilly, now let's see."

"There's a nice house in the village,
furnished with loving care."
His soft voice coaxed, persuadingly,
"Come, let me take you there."

Her sombre eyes looked up at him,
"It's here I want to stay."
"You'll love the house, and garden too,
It's not far from the bay."

So, they climbed the hill together,
and walked along the lane,
the sea behind, the fields before.
The sun replaced by rain.

They reached her rose trimmed cottage door,
far from the lapping sea.
A garden planted out with crops,
and table set for tea.

"Now Dilly, you have furniture,
and armchair by the fire.
There's crockery, and little bed,
to sleep on when you tire.

Oh yes! And there's a lovely clock
that's hanging on the wall.
So, you will know what time it is,
to make tea, when I call.

So, drink up now, and eat the food
Kind Mrs Gregg prepared."
But Dilly couldn't eat, or drink.
She simply sat and stared.

"I think I'd best be going back,
The sea is missing me."
"You'll love it here, and settle in
as happy as can be."

They left her.   Just a silhouette
against the bright fires glow.
With flickering shadows, images,
of things she did not know.

Voices and footsteps up the road.
Strange creaking in the hall.
All unfamiliar sounds to her,
replaced the soft seas call.

She told the time by sun and moon,
and did not need a clock.
It frayed her nerves. It never stopped.
That loud tick- tock, tick- tock.

She'd never felt alone before.
In fear she went outside.
No sound. A silent, sullen sea.
No lapping of the tide.

No tang of sea salt in the air,
just rotting leaves and mould.
This house was not a home for her.
She felt afraid, and old.

The road that led back to the bay,
was very long and steep.
That lonesome sea, she heard it moan,
sighing in its sleep.

She struggled on against the wind.
Sea music filled her ears.
The sea women were calling her,
"I'm coming home my dears"

She reached the stile above the cliff,
moonlight upon the shore,
Her cottage, with its ruined thatch
And sea pinks 'round the door.

Such joy!   A great sob tore her throat,
"My dears I have come home!"
Her dimming eyes saw far below
pale arms wave from the foam.

She watched them gleaming in the spray,
and listened to them croon,
and saw, again, the child folk play
beneath the waning moon.

She hurried down onto the shore
the waves were flecked with white.
A cry resounded round the bay.
A cry that rent the night!

With daybreak, came the mournful call
Of seagulls in the bay.
The sad sea roared.   The strong wind howled.
Sea women wept all day.

Against the stones, lapped little waves,
Far out a curlew cried.
Dilly, with sea pinks in her hand,
beside her door, had died.

Chapter 9 - Allusion

A brief, intentional reference to a historical, mythic, or literary person, place, event, or movement. "The Waste Land," T. S. Eliot's influential long poem is dense with allusions. The title of Seamus Heaney's autobiographical poem "Singing School" alludes to a line from W.B. Yeats's "Sailing to Byzantium" ("Nor is there singing school but studying /Monuments of its own magnificence").

The Elysian Fields

by Agnieszka Dryjas- Makhloufi

When your senses are paralysed
but your numb fingers still
want to play a game with life.

When your heart freezes
but your lips still miss touch.

When you can't walk further
but desire to move
is stronger than that.

When your foot sinks in the Elysian Fields
but another one caresses the warm ground.

You are still alive!

Harry Potter's Quidditch Jockstrap

by H.B. O'Neill

Ebay is my enemy and that's why I'm awake at 3 am.
18 bids a twitchy finger and no Buy It Now
Heart thumping as the countdown concludes
Harry Potter's quidditch jockstrap
Authentic sweat and an errant hair

Purchase the narrative as much as the leather
An included photo that's blurred but enticing
Gryffindor's greatest on his Nimbus 2000
Taut sleek buttocks and a cold steely grasp
Mother's Christmas made and Aunty Jean jealous

Non, Je Ne Regrette Rien

by Mary L Walsh

Regrets; consign them to the tomb
Deny the pointless energy spent
LIVE, BREATHE and GRAB life's ragged path
Only kindness matters at its end
In life's rich dance.
Kristofferson sang of
Trading his tomorrows for a single yesterday
Strikes a chord,
Regret for things undone
Plays eternal round
Futile energy spent on time and tide
A backward look a fervent glance
Things thrown away on little chance
Unless there is something you can do
To right the wrongs, dispel the gloom?
Regrets; consign them to the tomb and
LIVE!

Heartfelt

by Mary L Walsh

I stand here like Lady MacBeth
Hands, blood covered
Heart filled, after life stuffed with herbs
Festooned with the tears of onions
Sweetness of carrot
Cleaning the debris of lives once lived.
In fields of green......

Don't fret, just braised hearts for tea.

Grownups

by Jenny Grant

So here we are, shocked by sudden death
finally acting like grownups, clinging
to each other in the dark and afraid
for the first time that we won't live forever.

Scared that one day there won't be
another chance to embrace
to feel loved and close like this, our
arms wrapped around each other

clinging tightly like we're shipwrecked
being tossed about at sea.
It's a time of tenderness and sorrow.
I love you more because I can see how

lost you are without your friend Balder.
So, we talk of funeral plans, and saving up,
life insurance, film tickets, meerkats.
It's all bollocks really.

What would happen if one of us
should die, all the practical things.
Bank accounts. The skeletons
in your closet, the buried remains

of what you leave behind, I really
can't face having to unravel
your big legal mess and cope
with losing you at the same time.

I imagine you, entering Valhalla
as your Viking longship burns
arrows flaming in an arc
setting fire to the black sails

your silent body lying
on a pile of furs, holding your war axe
and longsword, your shield
and golden torch glowing with firelight.

Gratitude

by Agnieszka Dryjas-Makhloufi

To touch this sacred land
by my feet.
To hold its blooming bosom
it's a miracle.
To play on the strings of wind
and carry beautiful life stories
in my heart.
To gasp in wonder when looking
how the sky blushed
and how the Divine's hand painted the trees
again this spring
it's a miracle.
To feel how more and more
in love with life I am.
How the sunrays caress my cheeks,
to hear my mother's voice reaching
me from over the miles.
Sweet kisses from husband
falling like rose petals on my face.
Thousands of smiles from
the strangers' faces.
It's a miracle
to breathe and sink in your own heartbeat,
flowing with words of poetry.
To measure happiness by rain droplets.
To smell the whole kingdom of roses.

It's a miracle
to dance on a bare ground and feel connection
with the sweetest spirit of Mother Earth.
To feel it's every part in oneself,
her every part in yourself,
to carry her smile on the face,
to inhale her breath.
It's a miracle.

Chapter 10 - Epistolary Poems

Epistolary poems, also called verse letter or letter poems; are poems in the form of an epistle or letter.

Epistolary poems date at least as early as the Roman poet Ovid (43 BC – 17 or 18 AD), who wrote the Heroides (The Heroines) or Epistulae Heroidum (Letters of Heroines), a collection of fifteen epistolary poems presented as though written by a selection of aggrieved heroines of Greek and Roman mythology, addressing their heroic lovers who have in some way mistreated, neglected, or abandoned them.

Letter to Tiredness

by Mary L Walsh

You, Tiredness, visit me all my working days
I drag my weary aching feet home
An eight-hour day behind me
Carrying loaded bags of shopping
to a house where dinner needs to be cooked
the children need love and attention,
Sometimes I neglect them because of you, Tiredness.
Cleaning, washing, ironing, and always you, Tiredness
Why don't you not take a day off, Tiredness?
You weary the very soul of me.
I cannot carry everything and you,
You are always present, from my waking until my last thought,
You weigh down my spirit with your demands.
To sleep, a month or more may make you leave me
You persist, like a constant toothache
Forcing me to ignore you
To carry you like a burden
Until Collapse comes to
change shifts with you.

Lost

By Jenny Grant

I am in a different world
since you left.
Less light, less colour.
I lost my innocence.
Nothing tastes like it used to.
I have no thirst.
Instead of sleeping, I miss you
and lie awake, aching.
Tears slide down my cheeks
in lines to my pillow, damp.

The night folds into dawn
and seasons change
Christmas is less jolly
I put away my tree
and fill the void with wool
No decorations, fruit cake
or cheese biscuits, no port.
New Year turns up, I am asleep at 10.
There's no-one to call and wish at midnight.
Are there fireworks somewhere?

Winter lingers cold over the house
and spring is late.
I miss the way you smell.
I long to hold you again.
I want to look into your eyes
and see your smile. Where are you?
Somewhere in my house?
In the garden?
You're in another room perhaps
and I'm panicking.

Just sitting with you felt like peace
you were enough.
Holding your hand
sharing the room's breath with you.
Content, comfort, gentle completeness
I open my mouth
to talk to you now and
there is no sound.
My lips part
and close again.

I long to reach out for you still.
Where did you go
why can't I be with you?
I don't understand
my life now or the new
shape of the world.
I make new friends
I dress, I laugh, I please myself.
I go out, I see things.
But you were my picture frame, my lens.

I feel so empty
I want to give everything I own away.
Empty all the rooms
so I can be sure you're not hidden someplace. I want to lose myself
so I can be lost with you.
Perhaps lost is a real place
so we should wait there together
and if someone finds me
they might find you and bring us both home.

A Letter To a Husband On Dreary Days

By Agnieszka Dryjas- Makhloufi

My dear,
Sometimes your
overcast face
tells me more than life.
My lips quiver and utter
your name.
In our cuddles
the world slows down.
Placing my tired face
on your lap,
I try not to say anything.
Silence plays on the strings
of our hearts.

We keep repeating our mantra:
There are better days to come,
there are better days to come.
The drowsy moon sheds its light
illuminating our faces.
We are so helpless
clutching to the last crumbs of the day.
Shouldn't we let it go?
Let it go with all broken promises
and expectations.
I can hear your heartbeat now.
Dancing in the rhythm
of your accelerating pulse
I know myself more than ever.

Daughter, Mine

By Jenny Grant

Not every day will be filled with light.
You'll have sunny days you can't face
when your heart is full of gloom.
There will be worry and difficulty.
Plenty of that, but you're precious.

You're the light in my world
I wove into your being so much love
you are literally priceless.
Scorn the ones that try to break your heart
it is an ocean, boundless, magical.

Do not be afraid of life
All those twisty turns, the scary helter-
skelter, the speed of all the change
The disappointments, the crushing defeats
they are nothing, you will never be defeated.

You might think being good and having
such a big heart is a burden and a curse
But it is a rare blessing to be truly alive
And you burn like a flaming sword.
You are truth and justice, remember that.

Imagine yourself as a small hearted
person. What would it be like?
Pale passions, ignoble actions, shallowness.
You would be remote and lofty, too important
to be bothered with a small thing like love.

Doing the right thing sometimes hurts more
than letting others ride roughshod, trampling us.
You could never do a bad thing, it simply isn't in you.
I believe in you, and your pure heart and your patient
kindness. Oh gentle child. Daughter, mine

Letter to a friend on Seeing the Balcon Guitarist in Nerja, Andalusia

by Mary L Walsh

Dear Friend

I heard the sound of Spanish rhythms as I walked through the town
The percussive beat of footsteps echo along the Balcon
Rhythmically joined by the clap of pigeon and vibrant lush parakeet wings
The sun spread its warming tendrils across the azure Mediterranean sky
Lighting the supple verdant palm fronds
The Spanish guitar breaks through
"Rasgueado Alapūa" resonates
Waking the spirit of Lorca and Andalusia
The guitarist sits, his long fingers coaxing life from the strings
He is lost in his musical world, transported to a higher plane.
Unaware of the constant tide of tourists and bag sellers passing by.
He plays "Toque Airoso" His long hair sways in tempo.
His jeans torn at the knees that are crossed, cradling his guitar
I stand transfixed by the music of Spain and the "Toque Virtuoso"

I may remain here still

Your friend

Chapter 11 - Elegy

An Elegy is a poem or song written in honour of someone deceased.

It typically laments or mourns the death of the individual.

Elegy is derived from the Greek work elegus, which means a song of bereavement sung along to music played with a flute.

Lost with Glimpses

By Mary L Walsh

Thousands of tiny glimpses remind me of you, mum
Nothing fills the void left by your absence,
In dying you left me with fragments of memory
That fade away or burn bright at different times.
Emotions burst forth, anger at you leaving,
emptiness, loneliness and fear, acceptance sadness, love.
Even so my life and that of my sisters went on,
Altered beyond recognition.
The hub had left the house,
The catalyst that made us a family.
The linking love was gone.
Our only comfort looking back
Was that nothing worse would ever happen to us.
That day was like a heavy stone thrown into a pond
its ripples changed our lives in obvious and subtle ways.
Those ripples never stop,
They carry on washing over every aspect of our lives,
from then 'til now; forever

Deal Me In

By Jenny Grant

I'm not afraid to die Grandad,
I know you'll pull out a chair
And hand me a glass
And deal me into the game

Someone light me a cigarette
Joey the budgie is sitting on
Uncle Dave's shoulder, he's brazen
That bird, he's a cheeky boy

Nanny, how come you're finding
this fun, I've never seen you so relaxed
Oh, here's your Mam and Da,
Hello, give us a kiss

Right, so what am I betting on?
What's trumps? My glass is empty
again, who's got the bottle?
Harry, you're a devil, where did

That flush come from?
Jule, I'll dance with you later.
Listen to Stan playing that piano,
Who knew he could honky tonk?

All the old cats are sleeping
on the fur coats over the sofa, my old beast
is on my lap, and the brown one is by my feet.
Look at Sally, wagging her tail beside Grandad.

Elegy

by Agnieszka Dryjas-Makhloufi

Where are you now?

In every cherry tree I seek your smile.
Watching every sunset
I sigh and wipe my tears.
With the scent of the first flowers
I get drunk and dance
in the river of childhood memories.

We were playing hide and seek
chasing your cats,
showering the pups with kisses.
We were selling the grass in your garden,
pretending that it was chives.
The flames of burning fire
warmed up our hearts,
your fruit soup still lingers in my mouth.
So where are you now?

In every blooming cherry tree you smile.
After every sunset you rise in the sky
dressed in a purple cloud.
You shine brightly,
warming up my heart
like those flames of fire

Back to Blackbird

by Jenny Grant

When I heard you'd died, music poured out of me
I cried, inconsolable, missing you already, a part of me
had ended. The beautiful songbird I thought I'd befriended
although we never met. I was star struck, I loved the sad
in you, the soul of you, the lost and lonely broken heart I shared.

I was part of your music, you were part of me. It dealt
me quite a blow to think you'd gone for good, tragedy to lose
that stare, the lipstick, the thirst for drink you couldn't handle.

Your song came on the radio and I sung my heart out
Making up the words, well there's no one to care if I get it wrong
Just you and me and the melody, the trumpets, the volume
of the lungs of both of us like a karaoke against the world, you and me
well now it's just me against the music, wishing you were here.

Your voice was like honey and chocolate, in a good way, and
at the same time, you growled and soared and never missed a beat
Sublime crescendos of blues and swing, you were with me in the room
singing but someone left the window open and now the bird is gone.

Back to Black, and melancholy, you lifted my gloom and my heart
and I was up there with you, because of you, flying on your black
  wings,
aloft I knew someplace you'd be high, I didn't expect it to kill you
why did you drink to die, when there are better ways to live.

It's been years since, and the world is quieter, I don't mean
there's no roadworks or jackhammers in Camden , there's still
a racket; but there's a deathly silence now where once a lioness roared.

Dad

by Mary L Walsh

Last night I dreamt of Dad
The scent of tweed jacket
White of hair
Crinkle of twinkled eyes
Laughing together
We talked
I woke, eyes wet with tears
Sad for the reality of time.

Chapter 12 - Confessional

Confessional poetry is the poetry of the personal or "I."

This style of writing emerged in the late 1950s and early 1960s and is associated with poets such as Robert Lowell, Sylvia Plath, Anne Sexton, and W. D. Snodgrass.

Choosing Her Religion

by H.B. O'Neil

A clean-shaven Jesus
came enquiring at my door
Have you considered redemption?
My eyes dropped to the floor

If all of life is timing
(And I'm not saying that it's true)
Then his appearance seemed quite poignant
And all that followed quite the thing to do

He helped to hang the washing
I offered him some tea
He was in no apparent hurry
had no better place to be

That's what he said

I chose to take him at his word
somewhat in a state of awe
I rearranged my dressing gown
Then let the curtains draw

He offered manners and a sincerity
that were rare within these walls
He smiled an innocent agenda
and wasn't staring at my smalls

I asked to see his Bible
but he hadn't come prepared
Just leaflets and a magazine
Nice nostrils that soon flared

He was young and very trusting
Fully prepared to sit with sinner
I placed him in the dining room
Then carved a special dinner

Now if you practice what you preach
then I imagine there's no issue
As I drew the darkened knife away
I politely dabbed him with a tissue

He had knocked on many doors
So who knew where he'd be?
The man of faith is rarely missed
with all those souls to see

I hadn't planned a new addition
I'd thought I'd strike once only
But my chest freezer is a godsend
and one corpse might be lonely

A clean-shaven Jesus
came enquiring at my door
My husband worshipped Satan
Now neither boast no more

Realization

by Agnieszka Dryjas-Makhloufi

Swimming continuously in the river of life,
unaware of who I was, what I wanted,
I exerted myself and set my soul on fire.
It wept and wept, my tears
extinguished my pain.
My lips dropped the burden.
False masks were falling
like stones onto the ground.
Swimming in the river of life
I nearly sank
but emerged on the surface of truth.

Ghosted

By Jenny Grant

Folding the long, dark red evening gown with the beaded butterflies
on the bodice brought you back to me; it was you last wore that dress,
borrowed it to go to the opera in secret. You wore long evening gloves.
The vintage crepe dress was almost made for you, I didn't want to
  wear it
after you'd had it on. Unlike the other nice things you borrowed

you brought it back a few days later after leaving the bouquet
your creepy old man gave you, he liked you tied up in bondage and you
couldn't take those flashy flowers to your house because of your
  new bloke –
he might have burned his bridges leaving his wife and kids to be
  with you
(keeping the flashy car he was in debt for) but you always had other
  irons in the fire.

It was like being star struck, how I wanted to please you, and you took
advantage of me to the point where I felt completely used.
After being treated like some kind of idiot, told to lay on dinner
for all your friends on no notice something snapped. I was
disgusted with myself for putting up with you frankly. A rude
  awakening.

Funny, it was you said I was rude when we first met, when I thought
  no,
it was you was really off with me, and that wasn't how it was at all.
I stopped counting you as a friend whatever Facebook said months
  before
the vile text you sent me at work the day after your Dad died,
  throwing
my family in my face, despite knowing how much shame they
  caused me.

I'd already had enough so you didn't hurt me like you wanted to. I
  confess
I was glad I'd already decided to be shot of you. You're a total
  headfuck.

Ode to Cuisenaire® By Mary L Walsh

Oh Cuisenaire®, how could you dare
To ruin Maths without a care?
The boxes of coloured brick arrived
cornered in a classroom of
ignorance.
Exposed in all their coloured
brightness
Taken out for our maths lesson
A new and exciting innovation from
Belgium
A cure for working class lack of
maths ambition
bricks of different lengths and colours
White =1 through to Orange = 10.
After the lesson they were restacked
Soldier-like in the boxes
Colour segregated
Neat and clean
Though what they were supposed to teach me
I still do not know, their purpose lost
in a 60's progressive teaching nirvana
like phonetic reading of Janet and John
With Antony Ryan I mixed them up
Placed dark green and purple (=10) under orange (10)
Settled yellow and red (=7) under black (7)
Once all the colours had been used
The top layer replaced in its neat smugness
we sat each day in anticipation of discovery

The boxes threatened us with their secrets
The coloured rods menacing and smug
with the knowledge we did not possess
mathematical strength in numbers
beneath the neat shiny top layer,
they no longer lived in segregated stacks
Colour by Colour
but were forced to mix in a cacophony of addition.
Until teaching allowed the calculator

The Wife, The Husband, Lord Jesus and The Devil

by H.B. O'Neill

A clean-shaven Jesus
came to my door
Have you considered redemption?
My eyes fell to the floor

If all of life is timing
(And I'm not saying that it's true)
Then his appearance was quite poignant
And it seemed the thing to do

He had a pamphlet and sincerity
that were rare within these walls
He smiled an innocent agenda
and wasn't staring at my smalls

He helped me wheel the dustbin
I offered him some tea
He was in no hurry
had no better place to be

That's what he said

I chose to take him at his word
Still in a state of awe
I rearranged my dressing gown
Then let the curtains draw

I asked to see his Bible
but he hadn't come prepared
Just leaflets and a magazine
Nice nostrils that soon flared

If you practice what you preach
then surely there's no issue
As I drew the knife away
I offered him a tissue

He had knocked on many doors
So who knew where he'd be?
The man of faith is rarely missed
with all those souls to see

I hadn't planned a new addition
I'd thought I'd strike once only
But my chest freezer is a godsend
and one corpse would be lonely

A clean-shaven Jesus
came to my door
My husband worshipped Satan
Now neither boast no more

Chapter 13 - Sestina

A **sestina** also known as sestine, sextine, sextain) is a fixed verse form consisting of six stanzas of six lines each, normally followed by a three-line envoi.

The words that end each line of the first stanza are used as line endings in each of the following stanzas, rotating in a set pattern.

The invention of the form is usually attributed to Arnaut Daniel, a troubadour of 12th-century Provence, and the first sestinas were written in the Occitan language of that region.

The form was cultivated by his fellow troubadours, then by other poets across Continental Europe in the subsequent centuries; they contributed to what would become the "standard form" of the sestina.

The earliest example of the form in English appeared in 1579, though they were rarely written in Britain until the end of the 19th century.

The sestina remains a popular poetic form, and many sestinas continue to be written by contemporary poets. They are however, often considered quite challenging to write in view of the set pattern of the line endings.

Tussy Blue – the memories of Eleanor Marx

by Jenny Grant

There's nothing quite so dark as now where I am
Anyone can shine a light on me and that's the truth
Life is but a stage and there's a doll's house in my dream
Something's very wrong with the man that I love
Nobody doubt my foolishness, to be learned isn't wise
So I blindly wish for more from him, as ever

Come bring me kind smiles, one kiss will right me forever
Today my face is blue, for sad and gloomy I am
I know I shouldn't have gone along with you, it was unwise
And bitter aloes sour my mouth and that's the truth
But I'm not ashamed to be a fool, a fool for love
It's all a play, the lines are rehearsed, it's just a dream

So wake me darling, in my white dress, from this dream
Turn me round and hold me in your arms forever
I could never wish for more than your love
Happiness is next to you, any place that I am
Oh shut the door and open me to your dark truth
Kissing you's the only thing I've done that's wise

Looking outside at the rain, I regret I couldn't be more wise
So much longing poured forth as I reached out for my dream
In fact nothing could have turned out farther from the truth
And I am just as much alone with you as ever
Reflecting on how far I've fallen, and everything I am
I can't regret the stupid things I did for love

And yet, as I suffer for my agonising love
And wishing bitterly that I had been more wise
Longing for you to see me truly as I am
Realising I have conquered nothing in my dream
Knowing I will love you in my heart forever
Above every lesson given I have learned my truth

But what does anyone know about the truth?
And surely we are all blind fools for love
Love is but a flame that burns too hot to last forever
And fire burns a foolish person the same as the wise
Life's so brief, so fill me with love's hot fires in my dream
And make me patient to be the loving fool that I am

And knowing ever I lived to seek the truth
Reckless lover, I am ever seeking love
No-one wise would ever follow my dream.

Chapter 14 - Ghazal

A Ghazal is a poem that is made up like an odd numbered chain of couplets, where each couplet is an independent poem. Traditionally, this poetry form is said to originate in the Middle East.

The Ghazal has a refrain of one to three words that repeat, and an inline rhyme that precedes the refrain.

Lines 1 and 2, then every second line should have this refrain and inline rhyme, and the last couplet should refer to the author's pen-name...

Ghazal for Amber

by Jenny Grant

What was the world before you were born?

  A small, lonely place, my daughter

You are the sun and you fill me with light

  I am better for you, my daughter

Your eyes are gentle, full of trust and hope

  Your smile is all the stars, my daughter

Proud of your truthful soul, my heart lifts with joy

  You made me complete, my daughter

Wherever you go is my home

  I am with you forever, my daughter

The quiet moments with you, alone in my arms

  Bring precious contentment, my daughter

You bring me glory, as you speak up for the world's children

  My fierce lion cub, my daughter

Jennifer's truest friend, I would give you my life

  My song is for you, my daughter

Jennifer's Heart

By Jenny Grant

The night is dark, and the scented air is clear
The stars are shimmering in your hair so clear

I wait for you, beneath the moon, with longing in my soul
Are you in the shadows, waiting for the street to clear

Fire burns inside me, I can think of nothing else
My passion rages, my heart's desire aware and clear

Fly to me my darling, my forever love so true
The way into my warm embrace so rare and clear

Let there be no mystery, let us lie entwined
And I Jennifer, give you my heart to wear, so clear

Chapter 15 - Prose

Prose is so-called "ordinary writing" — made up of sentences and paragraphs, without any metrical (or rhyming) structure.

If you write, "I walked about all alone over the hillsides," that's prose. If you say, "I wandered lonely as a cloud/that floats on high o'er vales and hills" that's poetry. See the difference?

From prose we get the term prosaic, meaning "ordinary" or "commonplace," or lacking the special delicacy and beauty of its supposed opposite — poetry.

Afternoon with Dad

by Mary L Walsh

A wren, brown, speckled on the bare

Winter twigs outside the window

Inside quiet, tea made, and lunch served

The afternoon nap imminent

TV, sound off, subtitles on,

Cars thrum by in the street,

A plane overhead off to destinations unknown.

Paper being turned, examined for news.

The hour in the afternoon.

Jobs done

Until tea time

Peace.

Primus Inter Pares

by Jenny Grant

Underneath your smiling demeanour sits
a persistent hatred. In public, you have often
sympathised with me, your convenient agreement
conceals all your petty undercurrents.

I see her detain you at the end of Cabinet,
You're now talking together in a side room.
Pushing back my chair, I stride forward,
planning to forestall her. As I interrupt

your hushed confidences you startle; wearing
a flush of emotion. Others throng behind me
into the tiny room. Loud talk breaks out as I push
past them. Voices roll in the hall's great spaces.

There was a call for silence.

Head bowed, and despite the chorus of flashing lenses
I walk defiantly past the great panelled door
and down the curved marble steps.
The great numbered columns holding up the portico

seem to shrug. Broadcasters and microphones ring the vehicle
as I bend to get inside the waiting car. The shining doors close
with a click. I sink into the warm leather seats and bite my lip.
The driver doesn't need to be asked, he will take me home

Night Ritual

by Mary L Walsh

The moon, cream coloured and pancake like,
hangs among the stars
Tilly, our white highland dog stares up
her thinking hidden in deep meditation.
What does she see there in the midnight sky?
Stars, older than the earliest dogs, reflect in her eyes
older than the dogs domesticated when man needed companionship,
or to guard against intruders,
or to herd the cattle and sheep,
now he was no longer a hunter gatherer.

Stars older than the dogs worshipped in the form of Anubis
Twinkle in the vaulted cathedral of the universe as
Tilly conducts her nightly business
 then sits again at the edge of the patio
gazes heavenward, taking in the scent of the evening
What does she see there in the midnight sky?
What aromas meet her senses?
Later, in the quiet of the early hours, she tells me all
Sadly, I cannot translate.

Custom House

by Jenny Grant

Cold dawns in hoar frost
early daylight on grey skies
melt the night into a patch of tar
dissolve the moon as a slick of oil

Behind the old warehouse
warped lengths of timber lean
still smelling faintly of turpentine
roughly hewn, warped and knotted

Door creaks hinges protesting
gauges the floor where it's swollen
rain and neglect, nothing remains
nose ghosts of spices, rum, tea, and cigars

Rooftops still darkened from industry
smoke rises from chimneys into smog
black and indifferent, shuffling coats
shiny eye, cawing crows scatter

Biographies

Jenny Grant

Jenny Grant is a poet and artist and a ferocious knitter. She has spent her entire life making things and writing. For two years she has run the Barking Foxes Poetry Stanza. The house she lives in is haunted by her Nan and Grandad. She loves the scent of orange blossom and makes marmalade from a little orange tree on the windowsill. The love of gold and bright blue also leads her to suspect she is in fact Louis XIV. When not writing or making something, she might be loafing in the garden shed with the kitten horde.

Lucy Kaufman

Lucy Kaufman is a playwright and author. She studied Film & Literature at University of Warwick, where she waddled into her Finals nine months pregnant. Between babies, Lucy has had 27 of her plays performed professionally around the UK and Australia. Her maddest moment was writing a four-part WW1 musical and three short plays in one month. The shortest month.

Lucy's first novel Pretty Bubbles recently came 3rd in 'Pen to Print' competition. She is currently growing accustomed to rejection. Poetry was intended to be a bit of fun; it is as agonizing as her other writing.

H.B. O'Neill

H. B. O'Neill is a London born writer inspired by the City and its myriad opportunity for comedy, pain, irony, danger and adventure.

He is a prize winning short story writer, poet, screenwriter and playwright. His much anticipated debut novel is due to be published later this year.

Mary L Walsh

After spending most of her school days staring out of the window Mary developed a keen imagination, this helps her write poems on all subjects from making dinner to falling over in the garden. She writes for her children and grandchildren and they each have their own handwritten books. Mary has really enjoyed developing her skills with the Barking Foxes. She lives in Essex, with her husband Denis, Dog Tilly, Cat Theo and a canary named Mr. Pickles.

Robert Drury

Robert retired some thirty years ago from active Missionary service. Those were the important years of his life. He has considered himself, in the past, to be a religious Christian activist but strictly, a political observer. He considers both subject to be important in the society of mankind.

He has also been a chef, computer consultant, waiter, hotel doorman and concierge. He wrote his first ever real poem on 25th May 2016. The story around why he wrote his first poem, he will be happy to express, anytime. His poetry is designed to take you to the edge, in some way, but not over the edge.

Agnieszka Dryjas-Makhloufi

Agnieszka comes from Poland. She has been living in the UK for 7 years. An English teacher by profession she used to work as a TA in primary and secondary schools in the UK. Currently she is an ESOL teacher. She has been writing poetry since she was 13. She loves expressing herself via various mediums such as writing, drawing, painting, sewing and many more. She practices mindfulness which helps her to live life in the present and her writing reflects this approach. Agnieszka is very passionate about writing poems, fairy tales and short stories.

Elizabeth Freeman

When she was young she had the wanderlust, so gave up her safe Civil Service job, for adventure. "If you wait for other people you never do anything, "she said. So off she went alone, and travelled, overland to India by bus, then by bus, and on to Nepal, Thailand, Malaya, Australia and New Zealand where she did seasonal work to get her fare home. This was via New Guinea, Hong Kong, Philippines, Taiwan and Japan. She visited Christian missionaries.

Finally, across Russia on the Tran Siberian Railway and home.

When she got back to England people, both young and old, wanted to hear her stories and see her slides. They gathered in Churches and houses to listen to these adventure tales, which emphasised how God had taken care of her in many situations, one being nearly sold as a slave in Iraq and how that ended. For her family, she's written down these tales of her time of adventure. After taking up teaching and bringing up her son she is now retired and lives with her family of four grandchildren. She thought she was settled down now, and so did everyone else, until one day the family went away on holiday. Something of that old adventurous spirit rose up in her again, after more than fifty years. "I'm not sitting here alone, thinking of my aches and pains. I've got my Rose of England bus pass. I'm off."

So, she went on the buses and travelled the land, from Berwick on Tweed back home. She likes researching people's lives and her new hobby is writing some of them as ballads. Other people's lives of adventure.

Eithne Cullen

Eithne Cullen was born in Dublin; her family moved to London when she was 6 years old. She has taught in East London secondary schools for 37 years. An avid reader, Eithne takes great pleasure from her reading group which encourages an eclectic mix of books. She likes to write stories and poems and is a member of Forest Poets, Write Next Door and Barking Foxes. She lives with her husband in East London, is unashamedly proud of her three grown up children and endeavours to embarrass them as often as she can.